D1052800

LOUISIANA PURCHASE

PETER ROOP & CONNIE ROOP

ILLUSTRATED BY SALLY WERN COMPORT

ALADDIN PAPERBACKS

New York   London   Toronto   Sydney

For La and Jake—Rock and Bowl Forever!
—P. R. & C. R.

First Aladdin Paperbacks edition October 2004
Text copyright © 2004 by Peter Roop and Connie Roop
Illustrations copyright © 2004 by Sally Wern Comport

ALADDIN PAPERBACKS
An imprint of Simon & Schuster Children's Publishing Division
1230 Avenue of the Americas, New York, NY 10020

Designed by Debra Sfetsios and Lisa Vega
The text of this book was set in Cheltenham.

Printed in the United States of America
2 4 6 8 10 9 7 5 3 1

Library of Congress Control Number 2004101181
ISBN 0-689-86443-4
ISBN 0-689-86445-0 (Library Edition)

TABLE OF CONTENTS

Cast of Major Characters

Thomas Jefferson: Thomas Jefferson, author of the Declaration of Independence and third president of the United States, dreamed of extending America's borders from the Atlantic to the Pacific. His concept became the driving force behind the Louisiana Purchase as well as the Lewis and Clark Expedition.

Napoléon Bonaparte: Napoléon Bonaparte was a French military leader who had become virtual dictator of France by 1803. Napoléon had dreams of conquering all of Europe, including his archenemy Great Britain. Napoléon declared himself emperor of France and almost accomplished his dreams of conquest. Napoléon's vision ended on the battlefield of Waterloo in 1815 when the British defeated Napoléon once and for all.

Robert Livingston: Livingston was a wealthy New York politician and skilled negotiator. President Jefferson sent Livingston to France to purchase the important port city of New Orleans. Livingston's diplomatic skills were severely tested by Napoléon and Talleyrand. In the end, Livingston prevailed and purchased not only New Orleans, but all of Louisiana.

James Monroe: James Monroe was a trusted friend of President Jefferson's. Jefferson, realizing that Livingston was having difficulties, sent Monroe to France to help purchase New Orleans. Together, Monroe and Livingston sealed the deal. Monroe became the fifth president of the United States. His famous "Monroe Doctrine" warned European powers (like France) to keep out of the affairs of North and South America.

Charles-Maurice de Talleyrand: Talleyrand

was a wealthy French aristocrat who served Napoléon as his foreign affairs minister. Talleyrand, who spent two years in the United States, had a poor opinion of Americans. Talleyrand was determined to keep the Americans out of the Louisiana Territory. Obviously, he failed.

Toussaint L'Ouverture: General L'Ouverture was called the Napoléon of the Caribbean. An ex-slave, L'Ouverture led a successful slave revolt which took control of the Caribbean island of Santo Domingo from wealthy French plantation owners. Through war, bribery, trickery, and outright lying, General L'Ouverture was captured by Napoléon's troops and taken to France, where he died in a prison cell. In the end L'Ouverture's dream triumphed. Today Santo Domingo is the home of independent nations Haiti and the Dominican Republic.

Charles Leclerc: Napoléon chose his brother-in-law General Charles Leclerc to conquer wealthy Santo Domingo. France had once ruled half of this island. After his victory in Santo Domingo, General Leclerc was to establish a military presence in Louisiana to keep out the Americans. Before he could achieve either goal, Leclerc was defeated and killed, not by a human enemy, but by a deadly disease-carrying insect: the mosquito.

Aedes aegypti: Female mosquitoes which carried the deadly disease yellow fever. Yellow fever wiped out one of Napoléon's most valuable armies on its way to Louisiana.

Meriwether Lewis and William Clark: Meriwether Lewis was President Jefferson's private secretary. Even before the Louisiana Purchase, Jefferson personally selected

Lewis to lead an expedition up the Missouri River in an attempt to find a water route across North America. Moody and brilliant, Lewis ably accomplished the mission President Jefferson had given him.

William Clark met Meriwether Lewis when they served together in the United States army. Lewis picked Clark, a skilled mapmaker and capable commander, to cocaptain the Corps of Discovery. Together, Lewis and Clark successfully completed one of America's greatest adventures.

NAPOLÉON TAKES
A BATH

APRIL 7, 1803. Napoléon, the ruler of France, settled into his hot bath. Napoléon enjoyed soaking in his steaming tub as he planned to conquer other countries. Already he had conquered parts of Europe. Now Napoléon set his eyes on the next prize: the island kingdom of Great Britain, less than twenty miles away from the French coast.

Scratch, scratch, scratch.

Napoléon had forbidden anyone to knock on his Paris palace doors. Everyone had to scratch like a cat in order to see Napoléon, the "Man of Destiny." Napoléon frowned at the interruption, but nodded to his servant to open the door.

Lucien, Napoléon's younger brother, marched in.

In a book about his life, Lucien Bonaparte described the following historic events, highlighting the conversations as he remembered them.

As Napoléon and Lucien talked about their childhood in Corsica, they heard, *scratch, scratch, scratch.* Another interruption!

"Let him come in," Napoléon said. "I will stay in the water a quarter hour longer."

This time Joseph, Napoléon's older brother, entered the bathing room.

Lucien bragged about the secret treaty he had just negotiated with Spain. Spain, which had owned Louisiana since 1763, had recently given Louisiana back to France.

Joseph and Lucien broke into a heated

argument about what to do with this vast Louisiana territory, far away in North America.

Joseph turned to Napoléon and asked, "Well, you still say nothing of your great plan?"

Napoléon answered from the comfort of his perfumed bath.

"Oh! Yes," Napoléon stated. "Know merely, that I have decided to sell Louisiana to the Americans."

Tempers flared.

Lucien squeaked, "Ah! Ah!"

Joseph snapped at Napoléon, saying the French government would not support selling such a valuable French asset.

Napoléon stood, then remembered he was naked and plopped down in his bathtub. Water showered Joseph. The servant, overcome by the scene, fainted.

Napoléon abruptly ended the discussion.

"And then, gentlemen, think what you please about it, but give up this affair as lost to both of you. I shall get along without the consent of anyone whomsoever, do you understand?" he exclaimed.

Napoléon, the most powerful man in France, had made up his mind. He didn't want the tremendous expense of governing the Louisiana Territory. He urgently needed money for his European wars. He especially wanted to invade Britain. (Ironically, British banks also loaned money to Napoléon, money which he planned to use to conquer Britain.)

Selling Louisiana would solve both problems.

But only if the Americans would purchase Louisiana.

WHAT WAS THE BIG DEAL ABOUT LOUISIANA, ANYWAY?

THREE THOUSAND miles away in Washington, D.C. (most of which was still being built), President Thomas Jefferson was trying to buy just New Orleans, not all of Louisiana.

In 1803 the young United States extended from the Atlantic coast to the Mississippi River. President Jefferson dreamed of the energetic United States spreading west across the Mississippi River, stretching "from sea to shining sea." However, Jefferson's vision of pioneers settling the heartland of North America west of the Mississippi seemed almost impossible. Louisiana was so vast, and now it was owned by the French.

That spring, however, Jefferson desperately wanted New Orleans. This vibrant city, one hundred miles from the mouth of the Mississippi, controlled shipping on the mighty river. Three out of every eight bushels of corn grown in America passed through New Orleans. Three out of every eight American hogs sailed through New Orleans. Three out of every eight bundles of American furs were transported through New Orleans. The products bought, sold, and delivered were worth millions of dollars to Americans.

If New Orleans became an American port, the farmers in the current states and future states of Ohio, Pennsylvania, Kentucky, Tennessee, Indiana, Illinois, and Mississippi would shout for joy. And vote for Jefferson again.

If Jefferson couldn't buy New Orleans, the western settlers threatened to declare independence, leave the United States, and create their own nation. Who could understand this threat better than President Jefferson, who had written the Declaration of Independence?

If the United States owned New Orleans, however, no country could ever block the valuable river trade.

Jefferson wrote, "There is on the globe one single spot, the possessor of which is our natural and habitual enemy. It is New Orleans through which three-eighths of our territory must pass to market."

Jefferson continued, "The day that France takes possession of New Orleans . . . we must marry ourselves to the British fleet and nation."

This was a complete about-face for America.

French aid in the Revolutionary War had enabled the United States to defeat Great Britain and gain its independence. Now the relationship between France and the United States was in trouble. France, in a state of revolution herself, had been harassing American ships and sailors. The two countries were so close to war that George Washington came out of retirement to organize an army.

Things had settled down by 1800 as Napoléon gained power and focused his energies against European countries and not America.

But Napoléon certainly didn't want the United States to ally itself with his archenemy, Great Britain. Together, the two nations might thwart his dreams of conquest.

With Spain on his side, however, Napoléon could accomplish his visions of empire.

Since 1763 Spain had been the proud owner of the Louisiana Territory.

Nobody knew the exact borders of Louisiana. On most maps it stretched from Canada to Texas, from the muddy Mississippi to the snow-capped Rocky Mountains. These boundaries, however, were sketchy.

In 1800, in a secret treaty, Spain traded Louisiana to France. In return Spain received Tuscany, a prosperous region of Italy.

Spain was glad to let France have Louisiana. The territory cost too much to govern. Spain also didn't want the United States to possess Louisiana. This would put the grasping Americans too close to Spain's rich Mexican gold and silver mines. A French Louisiana would keep the eager Americans at bay. Or at least, east of the Mississippi.

The Spanish felt they had bested Napoléon.

Beautiful, wealthy Tuscany for a worthless, deserted wilderness.

The wilderness, however, was not worthless. Nor was it deserted.

Louisiana was home to thousands of Native Americans. The Sioux, Iowa, Blackfeet, Cree, Shoshoni, Kansas, and dozens of other tribes lived in Louisiana. Here they laughed and cried, lived and died. They hunted, they traded, and they fought one another.

Millions of buffalo, elk, deer, and antelope roamed the vast plains and mountains. Grizzly bears scavenged. Prairie dogs dug underground dens. Ducks, pelicans, geese, and cranes flocked. Hawks, falcons, and eagles soared. Lakes, rivers, and streams teemed with beaver, muskrats, and fat fish. Thriving prairie grasses waved in the winds. Birch, pines, aspens, and cottonwoods grew tall.

Far away on another continent, a dripping Napoléon made the decision that would change the people and environment of Louisiana forever.

3

THE DEAL IS SEALED

WOULD THE United States really buy Louisiana? Napoléon wondered.

President Jefferson and Congress had already told Robert Livingston, the United States minister to France, to buy New Orleans. Congress approved two million dollars to purchase the valuable "Crescent City." Jefferson secretly told Livingston to go as high as ten million dollars.

By 1803 Livingston's negotiations were beginning to bear fruit. The French were indeed interested in selling New Orleans.

Imagine Livingston's surprise when on April 7, 1803, four days after Napoléon's interrupted bath, France offered not just New Orleans to the United States, but all of Louisiana, too!

Livingston said the United States was only interested in New Orleans.

But he was curious. What would all of Louisiana cost? Livingston offered France twenty million francs, or five million dollars, for New Orleans and Louisiana together.

Much too low, laughed Talleyrand, Napoléon's Foreign Affairs Minister.

Two days later, President Jefferson's trusted friend, James Monroe, arrived in France to aid in the negotiations. Monroe's arrival upset Livingston because he was so close to picking the plum of New Orleans by himself.

With Monroe by his side, however, Livingston now had more power to negotiate.

France and the United States argued over the price. Finally, they settled on sixty million francs (about fifteen million dollars).

What a bargain!

Less than four cents an acre for each of Louisiana's 375 million acres! Louisiana was 828,000 square miles (2,144,486 square kilometers) and doubled the size of the United States!

Monroe and Livingston now had a complicated problem on their hands. President Jefferson and Congress had told them to buy New Orleans. The president had said nothing about all of Louisiana.

Monroe and Livingston knew it would take months to send word by ship to President Jefferson and receive his reply.

They couldn't pass up such an incredible deal. No problem, they told Talleyrand. The United States would pay the fifteen million dollars.

Monroe and Livingston had no idea how

they would get the money. Ultimately, it was borrowed from Dutch banks.

Regardless, on May 2, 1803, Monroe and Livingston signed the historic treaty to purchase Louisiana. After signing, they shook hands with Napoléon. Livingston said, "This is the noblest work of our whole lives. From this day the United States take their place among the powers of the first rank."

Napoléon was extremely pleased. With fifteen million dollars, he could pursue his plan to completely conquer Europe, then Great Britain.

Meanwhile, back in the United States, President Jefferson was hatching a plan of his own. He had persuaded a reluctant Congress to give him twenty-five hundred dollars to fund an expedition to secretly explore Louisiana.

Two years earlier, Jefferson had already

put part of his plan into operation. In 1801, after his election as president, he hand-picked Meriwether Lewis to be his personal secretary. Lewis, a family friend, experienced soldier, and avid woodsman, was to lead a "Corps of Discovery." Now, Lewis and his corps would explore Louisiana—without permission from the French. This was illegal and dangerous.

President Jefferson had no idea that, as Lewis prepared to leave for Louisiana, Louisiana actually belonged to the United States!

They both soon learned the historic news.

On July 4, 1803, the United States celebrated her twenty-eighth birthday. President Jefferson had another reason to celebrate this holiday. The night before, he learned that the United States had purchased

Louisiana! Jefferson realized that the nation he helped create in 1776 was now twice as big as it had been on its first birthday.

Jefferson was relieved. With New Orleans and Louisiana as part of the United States, no foreign power could stop traffic on the Mississippi. Jefferson wrote, "This removes us from the greatest source of danger to our peace."

Jefferson had a third reason to especially enjoy this Fourth of July. The next day Meriwether Lewis, at Jefferson's command, was to leave Washington and start preparing for his exploration of Louisiana to the Pacific Ocean. Now Lewis's expedition into Louisiana would be legal because the United States owned the territory.

Horatio Gates, a friend of Jefferson's, told him that the purchase of Louisiana "must strike every true friend to freedom in the United States as the greatest and most beneficial event that has taken place since the Declaration of Independence."

At first, President Jefferson thought the United States Constitution might not allow him to buy new land. The Constitution stated that the president could negotiate treaties with foreign nations. The Constitution did not state whether a president could buy land. After careful consideration, President Jefferson reasoned that, because the Louisiana Purchase was a treaty between the United States and France, he did indeed have the constitutional power to purchase Louisiana. Jefferson, however, said he "stretched the Constitution until it cracked."

Congress agreed with President Jefferson and ratified the treaty to purchase the Louisiana Territory.

On October 21, 1803, President Thomas Jefferson signed his name next to Napoléon's on the treaty. The deal was sealed.

A major milestone in the history of the United States had been reached.

4

WHAT EXACTLY DID JEFFERSON PURCHASE?

HAD PRESIDENT Jefferson really gotten a bargain? Or had Napoléon tricked the Americans into buying a worthless wilderness with no boundaries?

After purchasing Louisiana, the American minister Robert Livingston asked the French minister Talleyrand exactly where the borders were.

Talleyrand laughed.

"I can give you no direction," he smirked. "You have made a noble bargain for yourselves, and I suppose you will make the best of it."

In 1803 no one knew the exact boundaries of the vast Louisiana Territory. There was one boundary, however, everyone agreed upon. The Mississippi River was the eastern border of Louisiana. However, there was a small problem. No one knew where the Mississippi River began. So even this border was unknown.

Just what was this Louisiana which so many countries were trying to outwit one another to keep, steal, sell, or buy?

For the Native Americans, Louisiana was home. There were no borders in their Louisiana. The Iowa, Wichita, Comanche, Kiowa, Arapaho, Kansas, Osage, Missouri, Pawnee, Sioux, Mandan, Hidatsa, Crow, Gros Ventre, Ojibwa, Cheyenne, and dozens of other tribes roamed the vast territory. They built villages. If a tribe was strong, it might push a weaker tribe to another place. But there was room for all.

The Native Americans didn't know that Spain, France, and eventually the young United States claimed their lands.

How could these countries claim Louisiana?

European claims began in 1492 when Christopher Columbus reached the Americas. Columbus claimed the lands he encountered for Spain. It didn't matter to Columbus that Native Americans were already living here.

Word of Columbus's voyages quickly spread throughout Europe. Other countries wanted to claim land here, too. England, France, Holland, and Portugal sent expeditions to this so-called New World. Some of these explorers came for adventure. Some came to convert the Native Americans to

Christianity. Some came to find a new life. Almost everyone came to get rich. Fast.

Tales were told of mountains of gold and silver. Plus, there were Indians that could be enslaved to do the hard work of digging, hauling, and melting the gold and silver to ship home to the Old World.

The country which claimed the most territory would become the most wealthy. And powerful.

No one thought to ask the Native Americans how they felt about this invasion of their homelands.

For a few years after Columbus, the Spanish claimed the most land. First, they took islands in the Caribbean. Then they claimed Mexico. Next came Florida. In their greedy eyes, Florida meant all of North America!

The Spanish sent more explorers to find out just what they had.

In 1519 Alonso de Pineda sailed along the shores of the Gulf of Mexico. Pineda's expedition was the first from Europe to see the mouth of the mighty Mississippi. Pineda wrote home telling of the glories he had seen (and many he had imagined).

Such glorious news inspired Panfilo de Narvaez to set sail in 1528. Three hundred eager soldiers joined him. His treasurer, Alvar Cabeza de Vaca, came along to keep track of the riches they hoped to discover.

The expedition landed in Florida with high hopes. They enthusiastically marched west, but swarming bugs devoured them. Slimy mud gripped their feet. Rain showers soaked them. Hungry alligators snapped at them. Stifling heat steamed them.

And all the while they wore heavy metal armor in case of attack by the Native Americans.

For eight long years no one heard a word from the vanished expedition. Then, one day in 1536, Cabeza de Vaca and three other Spaniards staggered out of the wilderness. Every other man, including the leader Narvaez, had perished.

This New World was no heaven. More like the opposite. The men had claimed the land for Spain, but they weren't going to live there.

Cabeza de Vaca, however, wrote wonderful things about his horrible experiences. He described riches beyond belief. Somehow, he failed to mention the bugs, mud, rain, alligators, heat, and Native Americans.

News of such easy wealth inspired Hernando de Soto to try his luck. De Soto left his comfortable job as governor of Cuba. Six hundred excited soldiers joined him. They, too, marched west across Florida.

The same bugs, mud, rain, alligators, heat, and Native Americans attacked them. Finally, in May 1541, De Soto and what was left of his band reached the eastern shore of the rolling Mississippi River.

De Soto was not going to let the powerful river stop him from reaching riches. The determined Spaniards built boats and crossed the broad, brown Mississippi. In doing so they made history, becoming the first Europeans to walk west of the Mississippi.

De Soto didn't live to enjoy his fame. The next year he died after being bitten by a tiny mosquito which carried the deadly yellow fever. His men now numbered fewer than two hundred. They were hungry, tired, lost, and sick. They were under attack by the Native Americans who didn't want these invaders tramping across their lands.

The remaining men built boats and sailed down the Mississippi River, back to Cuba. Leave the land to the bugs, mud, rain, alligators, heat, and Native Americans, they said.

5

THE FRENCH CLAIM
AND NAME LOUISIANA

MEANWHILE, THE French were making their own plans. They had an idea. Since the Spanish were strong in the south, they would explore America from the north. Samuel de Champlain, governor of New France, now known as Canada, wanted to know what lay to the west and south.

The St. Lawrence River became the French highway into the heart of the continent. Traveling along the St. Lawrence, the French reached the Great Lakes. They crossed them in their swift canoes (invented by the Native Americans).

In 1634 Champlain sent his young friend

Jean Nicolet to explore the west. He wanted Nicolet to find riches, to claim more land for France, and to find a way across North America to China. With this goal in mind, Nicolet packed colorful Chinese clothes to wear to impress the Chinese he hoped to find.

One day in 1634 an excited Nicolet put on his Chinese robes. With a pistol in each hand Nicolet stepped ashore in today's Wisconsin and fired his pistols. *Bam! Bam!* the guns thundered.

Nicolet was just as surprised as the Native Americans he met. They wondered who Nicolet was, dressed in colorful robes and with thunder in his hands.

Nicolet wondered where he was, too.

Still, Nicolet claimed the unknown land for France before hurrying home.

But before he left, the Native Americans

told Nicolet about a great river farther to the west. They called this river *Mississippi.*

In 1661 Louis XIV became king of France. Louis was so vain that he compared himself to the glory of the sun. His countrymen called him "The Sun King."

The Sun King didn't want the bothersome Spanish anywhere near his New France. And he didn't want the annoying English anywhere near his French colonies. So he ordered more French explorers to head west and claim more land for France.

In 1672 Louis Joliet and Father Marquette set out to please the Sun King. Joliet knew his way around the American wilderness. He had traded with the Native Americans before. He dressed and lived much like them too. Plus, Joliet was skilled at drawing maps. He would map the lands he claimed so everyone would know just what the French owned.

Father Marquette was a Catholic priest. Like Joliet, he liked adventure. He would bring the Catholic religion to the Native Americans he met along the way.

In 1673 Marquette and Joliet set out in sturdy canoes. They followed the trail Nicolet had blazed, but they pushed on farther. In July 1673 they reached the misty Mississippi.

Still eager for more adventure and more land, they paddled up the rushing river, claiming everything in sight for France. However, they never found where the Mississippi River began.

Joliet made a map of all this new French territory.

Before long a copy of Joliet's map fell into the hands of Robert de La Salle. A rich young Frenchman, La Salle wanted adventure, glory, and more riches. *What better way to get them than to go down the Mississippi?* he thought.

La Salle decided to become friends with the Native Americans. He would build forts for protection and trading. He would keep the sneaking Spanish and evil English out of the heart of America. And he would put a big smile on the Sun King's face.

So in 1678 La Salle ventured forth.

The Native Americans he met, however, did not agree with La Salle's plans to build forts on their land. They attacked him.

So La Salle paddled down the Illinois River to the Mississippi. Then down the Mississippi he raced. Along the way he claimed land on both banks of the river for France. When La Salle finally reached the mouth of the Mississippi, he stopped.

On April 9, 1682, La Salle put up a marker and a cross. He buried a lead plate bearing the arms of France. La Salle thought big. He claimed all "the seas, harbors, ports, bays, adjacent straits and all the nations, people, provinces, cities, towns, villages, mines, minerals, fisheries, streams, and rivers," for King Louis.

To honor King Louis, La Salle called this vast land "Louisiana." The Spanish were angry. Wasn't this so-called Louisiana really part of their empire of New Spain? After all, they had gotten there first. Neither side bothered about what the Native Americans thought.

The Spanish set out to stop La Salle. They sent eleven expeditions to track him down.

But they couldn't find La Salle. After all, Louisiana was huge! Having finished claiming and naming Louisiana, La Salle returned home to France with the good news. France had a new empire.

A few years later La Salle returned to Louisiana to build colonies to make sure the Spanish kept out of French Louisiana.

La Salle and his colonists sailed in four small ships for the mouth of the Mississippi River. La Salle planned to sail up the river and plant his colonies along the way. He would show the Spanish.

La Salle's luck ran out. He got lost, his ships missed the mouth of the Mississippi, and he landed somewhere on the Texas coast.

La Salle's men were sick, hungry, and tired. His men killed La Salle and buried him in an unknown grave in the wilderness somewhere west of the Mississippi.

La Salle had claimed Louisiana, but in the end Louisiana claimed La Salle.

6

FRANCE GETS KICKED OUT AND BRITAIN GETS THE BOOT

WHILE THE Spanish and French were claiming land, the British were busy too. They had landed on the Atlantic coast and decided to stay. They built colonies: Roanoke (1584; it mysteriously disappeared), Jamestown (1607), Plymouth (1620), and many more. Like beads on a necklace, the British strung their colonies along the Atlantic coast. They found what they wanted. No need to go wandering around in the wilderness claiming everything in sight.

Besides, the looming bulk of the Appalachian Mountains to the west provided the British colonists with a natural border.

The British prospered between the mountains and the ocean. Before long, however, there seemed to be too many people in the thirteen colonies.

All of that wilderness west of the mountains tempted British settlers. They were eager to carve new farms into this huge western wilderness.

The French and the Native Americans disagreed. They didn't want British pioneers settling on their lands.

Tensions rose between the British and Spanish on one side, and the British, French, and Indians on the other. In 1754 the French and Indian War exploded, sparked by an unknown young Virginian named George Washington.

When the bullets stopped flying, the French and Indians had lost. In 1763 France was forced to give Canada and the Ohio valley to the British. France also had to give Louisiana to the Spanish. This is why Spain could claim Louisiana in 1800, and Napoléon had to plot to get it back.

The Native Americans, however, lost the most as British settlers swarmed into their lands.

The victorious British were upset. The war had cost too much. King George III and Parliament decided to make the thirteen American colonies pay for the war.

The independent-minded colonists said no, the British couldn't tax them. Only Americans could tax Americans.

King George III and Parliament disagreed. *We will tax your paper, your books, your ink. Why, we will even tax your tea!* they told the colonists.

This displeased the colonists so much (along with other British actions) that on

July 4, 1776, the colonies declared their independence. They would be the thirteen United States. The eight bloody years of the Revolutionary War that followed finally convinced the British they were wrong and that the colonies should have their independence.

To settle the peace, the British gave the infant United States all the British lands from the Atlantic Ocean to the Mississippi. They kept loyal Canada for themselves.

By 1783 the British were gone from the Atlantic to the Mississippi.

The French were gone from North America.

Spain, however, held on to Louisiana and Florida. Something about the bugs, mud, rain, alligators, heat, and Native Americans still appealed to them.

When Napoléon came to power in France he wanted revenge on the British. He planned to first conquer Europe before conquering Britain.

To do this, Napoléon needed Louisiana back in the French empire. So he persuaded the Spanish to accept beautiful Tuscany for the Louisiana wilderness.

On October 1, 1800, Napoléon signed the secret Treaty of San Ildefonso with Spain. Spain received Tuscany. France now owned Louisiana again. In the treaty Napoléon also promised never to sell Louisiana to any other nation, no matter what the reason.

7

NAPOLÉON'S DREAM
BECOMES A NIGHTMARE

NAPOLÉON DREAMED that Louisiana would be the cornerstone of his empire in North America. Napoléon was determined that France regain the lands she lost during the French and Indian War. He planned to establish forts, farms, and ship-yards in Louisiana. His soldiers would keep the land-hungry Americans out. His farmers would provide food for his expanding over-seas empire. His navy would control ship-ping on the Mississippi River and the Gulf of Mexico.

With the heartland of North America under his control, Napoléon believed that the riches of Mexico and South America would fall into his grasping hands. With the wealth of two continents, Napoléon could easily conquer his archenemy, Great Britain. Napoléon believed that Great Britain wasn't really so great anyway.

To put his dream into motion, however, Napoléon first must have cash.

Talleyrand, Napoléon's Foreign Affairs Minister and advisor, suggested that Napoléon get this cash by conquering rich Santo Domingo.

The island of Santo Domingo had once been one of France's wealthiest colonies in the Caribbean. Plantations there produced tremendous quantities of valuable coffee, indigo dye, and sugar. Santo Domingo would be Napoléon's stepping-stone on the road to conquering the world.

The wealth of Santo Domingo, however,

had been produced by the backbreaking labor of hundreds of thousands of black slaves. In 1801 the slaves, under the brilliant leadership of General Toussaint L'Ouverture, took control of the island. The United States aided L'Ouverture by supplying his army with food, guns, and gunpowder.

Napoléon made up his mind to defeat General L'Ouverture and conquer Santo Domingo. He ordered his brother-in-law, General Charles Leclerc, to take twenty thousand soldiers, sail to Santo Domingo, and return the island to French rule. Napoléon was so sure of success that he sent his sister Pauline with her husband. Napoléon calculated it would take only six weeks to defeat L'Ouverture. After he won, General Leclerc was to sail to Louisiana and firmly establish France's claim to this vast territory.

Neither Napoléon nor Leclerc knew the

French army would easily be defeated. Ultimately, it wasn't the strength of General L'Ouverture's troops which did the damage. Instead, blood-sucking mosquitoes shattered Napoléon's idea of an easy victory.

Napoléon never knew it was lowly mosquitoes that turned his dream of conquest into a nightmare. Another one hundred years would pass before humans discovered that hungry *Aedes aegypti* mosquitoes carried the deadly disease yellow fever. On Santo Domingo, yellow fever, not General L'Ouverture's army, proved to be Napoléon's greatest enemy.

At first, things went well for General Leclerc. He lost some battles, but he won others. He bribed several of L'Ouverture's generals into switching sides and joining him.

Slowly, however, the French army was being whittled away. Soldiers complained of dizziness, then they vomited blood. Their skin turned yellow and they shivered from high fevers. Death mercifully ended the miseries of many. Some days yellow fever killed over one hundred soldiers!

Before long, only four thousand of the original twenty thousand soldiers of Leclerc's army were still alive.

Then Leclerc himself became ill. He died on November 2, 1802. With Leclerc's death, Napoléon's dream for Leclerc's army to establish French rule in Louisiana died too.

The answer became obvious. Even though France had owned Louisiana for just two years, Napoléon knew he couldn't keep Louisiana and beat Britain, too. He must sell Louisiana to the Americans.

Napoléon's hatred of Britain gave the United States the greatest land deal in world history.

8

THE STARS AND STRIPES
FINALLY FLY
OVER LOUISIANA

WHEN THE United States purchased Louisiana, the flag of Spain still flew over the territory. Napoléon had been so busy with other affairs that he had not officially taken control of Louisiana from Spain. He had the secret treaty saying France owned Louisiana, but France had no government there.

In order for the United States to own Louisiana, Spain must first officially turn control of Louisiana over to France. Then France would turn it over to the United States.

Early in 1803 Napoléon sent Pierre de Laussat to be the French governor of

Louisiana. Laussat arrived in New Orleans on March 16, 1803. News traveled so slowly in 1803 that Laussat had no idea that on May 2, 1803, the United States had purchased Louisiana and that he would soon be out of a job.

Napoléon sent word to Laussat that he was not going to govern. Instead, Laussat was to simply receive Louisiana from Spain. Then he would turn the territory over to the United States.

On November 30, 1803, in an impressive ceremony, the Spanish flag was lowered in New Orleans. This marked the end of Spanish rule. The French tricolor flag was raised, signaling that Louisiana was now French.

Even though Laussat governed for only three weeks, he made use of his limited time. He passed laws. He held parties, dinners, dances, concerts, church services, and celebrations. Champagne toasts were given for Spain, France, and the United States.

For three weeks the French flag fluttered over Louisiana until December 20, 1803. That beautiful, balmy day a special ceremony was held.

William Claiborne represented the United States government. He was to be the new governor. General James Wilkerson and his soldiers represented American military power.

French troops stood on one side of the Place d'Armes, today's Jackson Square. American soldiers faced them. A flagpole towered between them.

The Louisiana Purchase Treaty was read out loud in French, then English. Laussat told Claiborne and Wilkerson that, as Napoléon's representative, he was "transferring the country to the United States." He handed over the keys to the city of New Orleans, tied with ribbons in the French colors of red, white, and blue.

Claiborne thanked Laussat "on an event so advantageous to yourselves, and so glorious to united America."

The French and the Americans signed the transfer papers. Slowly, the French flag was lowered while the American flag was raised. The two flags stopped briefly side by side. Suddenly, a cannon boomed. The Stars and Stripes climbed majestically to the top of the pole as the French flag came down. Cannons roared as people cheered.

It was official! Louisiana was now part of the United States of America.

That afternoon Laussat capped off the celebrations with a party for more than 450 people. Toasts were made to Spain, France, and the United States.

"Finally," Laussat wrote, "the last toast was offered to the eternal happiness of Louisiana, as a salvo of sixty-three rounds of cannon came to an end."

When the last dance finished that night, the party was over. Now the United States had to find out what it had purchased.

9

LEWIS AND CLARK
EXPLORE LOUISIANA

P RESIDENT JEFFERSON had already begun seeking the answer to this question when he established the Corps of Discovery under the command of Captain Meriwether Lewis.

Jefferson told Captain Lewis that he was to explore the Missouri River and discover if a water route existed across the continent to the Pacific. He wanted Lewis to keep a detailed journal and to make accurate maps. Jefferson wanted the expedition to record "the soil and face of the country, the animals, the mineral productions of every kind, and the climate."

Lewis was also to learn all he could about the Native Americans and their customs. Jefferson wanted the Corps to treat the Indians in a peaceful, friendly way.

This was a tall order for one man to handle, so Captain Lewis asked his friend William Clark to join him on the expedition and to participate in "its dangers and its honors." Lewis added, "There is no man on earth with whom I should feel equal pleasure in sharing them as with yourself."

Clark agreed, saying, "This is an undertaking fraught with many difficulties, but my Friend I do assure you that no man lives with whome I would perfur to undertake Such a Trip. I join you with hand and Heart."

Thus the famous team of Lewis and Clark was born.

During the winter of 1803–04, Lewis and Clark picked those who would join them on their historic journey, including York, Lewis's personal servant, and Lewis's dog, Seaman. They needed men willing to endure years of danger, suffer unknown hardships, and obey the commands of captains Lewis and Clark.

Captain Clark wrote in his journal on May 14, 1804, "Set out at four o'clock P.M. and proceeded under a gentle breeze up the Missouri."

No one knew they wouldn't return for two long, eventful years.

The expedition struggled upstream against the powerful current of the Missouri. The men paddled, poled, and pulled their canoes and boat.

The expedition suffered summer heat and weathered terrifying storms. "Mosquitoes and ticks are exceedingly troublesome," Captain Lewis wrote. Despite the hardships, the men marveled at the beauty of this new territory of the United States.

Dutifully, Clark made detailed maps of the river as they wound their way west through today's states of Missouri, Iowa, Kansas, and South Dakota, and into North Dakota.

Lewis and Clark decided to spend the winter camped by a Mandan village in North Dakota. There the men rested and repaired their equipment. They hunted deer and buffalo. Lewis worked on his journal, Clark on his maps.

The captains knew ahead of them lay the most challenging part of their journey. They must trade for horses with the Shoshoni Indians and cross the Rocky Mountains.

But no one knew the Shoshoni language.

Charbonneau, a French trader, was hired by Lewis and Clark to serve as an interpreter to Indian tribes farther upstream.

Charbonneau asked if his wife, Sacagawea, could go along. At first Lewis and Clark said no because Sacagawea had just had a baby. But when they learned that Sacagawea was Shoshoni they quickly changed their minds. Sacagawea could help them bargain for the much-needed horses.

Sacagawea and her baby Pomp stepped onto history's stage.

On April 7, 1805, the Lewis and Clark Expedition continued on its way. Before heading into the unknown they sent President Jefferson male and female antelope skeletons; four buffalo robes; thirteen fox skins; a buffalo robe painted with scenes from an Indian battle; and cages of live prairie dogs, magpies, and prairie chickens.

Clark wrote in his journal that night that "We are now about to penetrate a country at least two thousand miles in width on which the foot of civilized man has never trod."

Despite wind, weather, prickly cactus, and grizzly bears, the expedition pushed on.

Finally the snow-covered Rocky Mountains came into sight.

As they neared the towering mountains Sacagawea grew excited. She recognized familiar landmarks and wondered if any of her family were still alive.

Lewis went ahead to meet the Shoshoni, but he had no luck trading for horses. The Shoshoni chief Cameahwait said his people needed their horses.

Lewis called Sacagawea to help him bargain with the chief.

Sacagawea suddenly burst into tears and hugged Chief Cameahwait. The stubborn chief was her brother!

With Sacagawea's help, the expedition got the horses they desperately needed.

The mountain crossing was long and dangerous, but at last the Americans reached the western slopes. They canoed down the Columbia River to the Pacific Ocean. When they finally reached the seashore Lewis wrote, "Great joy in camp. We are in view of the ocean, this great Pacific Ocean, which we have been so long anxious to see."

The men spent the winter preparing for the return trip. On March 18, 1806, the Americans turned east and began the journey back home to friends and family. The return trip was much faster.

Sacagawea, Pomp, and Charbonneau left Lewis and Clark when the Americans returned to the Mandan lands.

On September 23, 1806, St. Louis came

into sight. The Lewis and Clark expedition had traveled over eight thousand miles (12,870 kilometers), much of it within the boundaries of Louisiana.

Many people had given the Corps of Discovery up for lost. Lewis, Clark, and their hardy companions, however, proved them wrong. Only one man, Sergeant Floyd, died on the journey, and that was most likely from appendicitis.

The Corps of Discovery had successfully accomplished the mission President Jefferson had given them. They brought back journals, maps, and pictures. They collected plant, animal, rock, and soil specimens. They encountered fifty Indian tribes. They had become the first Americans to set foot on parts of Louisiana.

Most of the Louisiana Territory was still

unknown and would take years to explore, but the discoveries had officially and legally begun.

With the purchase of Louisiana, the much larger United States had many difficult new questions to ask and answer.

How would Louisiana be governed? What new states might be formed out of the huge territory? Would slavery be allowed in these new states, or would the states be free? What would happen to the Native Americans who inhabited much of the Louisiana Purchase?

UNDER MY WINGS
EVERY THING PROSPERS

PRESIDENT JEFFERSON was very pleased with the reports of Lewis and Clark. The Louisiana Purchase had been a great gamble, but it was worth it.

Jefferson's goal of a nation stretching from the Atlantic to the Pacific had taken a gigantic step forward. Instead of America facing east to Europe as it had done since colonial days, the United States now became a country moving west.

While Lewis and Clark were away exploring, other events were shaping Louisiana.

In 1803, when the American flag first flew over Louisiana, it was a land of diverse people.

Native Americans lived throughout the Louisiana territory. New Orleans had a population of ten thousand people: Americans, Europeans, free blacks, black slaves, Native Americans, Creoles (people of mixed races), and others. One writer said, "I doubt if there is a city in the world, where the resident population has been so divided in its origin, or where there is such a variety in the tastes, habits, manners, and moral codes of its citizens."

The Louisiana Purchase treaty agreed to admit the people of Louisiana into the "Union of the United States and as soon as possible according to the principles of the federal Constitution to the enjoyment of all the rights, advantages, and immunities of citizens of the United States."

Until new states could be formed out of the Louisiana Territory, the residents would have freedom of life, liberty, property, and religion.

In 1803 the artist John Boqueta de Woiseri painted a colorful picture of New Orleans under the protection of an eagle's wings. The eagle holds a banner reading UNDER MY WINGS EVERY THING PROSPERS.

In 1804 the first anniversary of the Louisiana Purchase was celebrated throughout the nation. In New York City a gigantic map of Louisiana was paraded around town. In cities, towns, and villages, grand speeches were made and fireworks rocketed into the skies.

Not everyone celebrated, however. The New England states complained that Louisiana would make the southern states, especially Virginia, stronger. The issue was not the land but how the land would be peopled. *Would the new states be free or slave?* was the question of the day.

Many New Englanders were so upset about slavery spreading into the Louisiana Territory that they threatened to leave the Union. The verbal battle lines were being drawn, battle lines that became real in the Civil War.

The State of Louisiana was admitted to the United States on April 30, 1812, exactly nine years after the Louisiana Purchase treaty was written. The treaty was dated April 30, though it was officially signed on May 2, 1803.

Louisiana, the eighteenth state, was a slave state.

People against slavery felt that, if the states carved out of the Louisiana Purchase allowed slavery, the slave states would take over the nation.

In 1819 the question seemed settled. In order to keep an even balance between slave states and free states, the Missouri

Compromise was reached. This agreement meant that two states would be admitted to the United States at a time, one free and one slave. In 1819 Maine joined the Union as a free state and Missouri entered as a slave state. The states were now even: twelve free, twelve slave. The Missouri Compromise, however, stated that any new states created from land north of what is now Arkansas's northern border would be free.

The Missouri Compromise held until 1861 when the southern states left the Union to form their own nation, one which allowed slavery. After the four long bloody years of the Civil War the slavery question was finally answered. The northern free states won the war and ended slavery in all of the United States.

As more Americans settled on the Louisiana Purchase lands, conflicts arose between the pioneers and the Native Americans already living throughout the territory. One of President Jefferson's dreams had been to create a safe haven for Native Americans in the Louisiana Territory. This dream, however, would not come true.

For many Native American tribes living west of the Mississippi River, contact with the Europeans had been a mixed blessing. The Indians had been able to trade furs for iron pots and pans, blankets, guns, steel arrowheads, and other objects. The Europeans also brought horses, which enabled many tribes to search larger areas for food than they had been able to cover on foot.

But with the Europeans came diseases like smallpox, which killed tens of thousands of Native Americans who had no immunity against these deadly diseases from Europe.

Wars broke out between Americans and

the Indians. The Americans often claimed land where Indians lived. The Indians fought back to keep their homelands. But weakened by disease and facing the overwhelming firepower of the Americans, many Indian tribes gave up their lands and moved onto reservations. These reservations grew smaller and smaller over the years as the Americans, hungry for even more land, cut into Native American land that was supposed to be protected.

Settlers' trails, like the Oregon Trail and Mormon Trail, were etched across Indian lands. These trails disturbed the great herds of buffalo, elk, and antelope upon which many Indians depended for meat. Thousands of pioneers passed through the Indian lands on their way west to California and Oregon. Many, however, settled and carved farms out of the prairies. Others steamed up the Missouri aboard steamboats.

In 1869, President Jefferson's vision of a path across the continent became a reality. He had sent Lewis and Clark to find a water way west, but they discovered there wasn't one. By 1869, however, chugging "Iron Horse" locomotives followed their tracks from the Atlantic to the Pacific. In seven days people could cross the continent, "from sea to shining sea."

All of these new settlers increased tensions with the Indians. The final battles came after the Civil War when thousands of soldiers and their families, both Union and Confederate, moved west to settle. Brave, determined Indian leaders like Sitting Bull and Crazy Horse tried to stop the flood of American pioneers. In 1876, when the United States was exactly one hundred years old, General Custer lost the Battle of Little Big Horn, or Greasy Grass, as the Indians called it.

The cry across the country was to end the Indian wars. More battles, large and small, were fought. Year after year, however, the Native Americans lost more than they gained. At last, in 1881, Sitting Bull surrendered. The people who first inhabited the Louisiana Purchase had lost the fight to keep their lands.

In 1907 Oklahoma was admitted into the United States. This was the last state to be created out of the Louisiana Purchase. It had taken over one hundred years for all of the lands of the Louisiana Purchase to become states.

When Napoléon splashed in his bath in 1803 and made his decision to sell Louisiana, no one knew how this would change

American history. The nation expanded west. A civil war was fought and slavery was ended. Thousands of Native Americans were forced to give up their homelands.

The Louisiana Purchase still impacts America and the world every day. Food grown on the plains is shipped around the world. Gold, silver, coal, timber, water, and minerals from the lands of the Louisiana Purchase are used by millions of Americans.

In 1803 Louisiana was purchased for fifteen million dollars. In 1803 fifteen million dollars worth of silver, about 433 tons, would have filled 866 wagons in a line stretching over five miles. Today Montana alone produces that much silver every year!

In 1803 there were about five million Americans. The Louisiana Purchase cost each one three dollars. Today it would cost trillions of dollars to purchase Louisiana.

With the help of Napoléon, President Jefferson, and a tiny mosquito, Louisiana was purchased and became a milestone of American history.

States Formed from the Louisiana Purchase:

Louisiana: 18th State. Admitted in 1812.

Missouri: 24th State. Admitted in 1821.

Arkansas: 25th State. Admitted in 1836.

Iowa: 29th State. Admitted in 1846.

Minnesota: 32nd State. Admitted in 1858.

Kansas: 34th State. Admitted in 1861.

Nebraska: 37th State. Admitted in 1867.

Colorado: 38th State. Admitted in 1876.

North Dakota: 39th State. Admitted in 1889.

South Dakota: 40th State. Admitted in 1889.

Montana: 41st State. Admitted in 1889.

Wyoming: 44th State. Admitted in 1890.

Oklahoma: 46th State. Admitted in 1907.

BIBLIOGRAPHY

Barry, James. P. *The Louisiana Purchase.*
New York: Franklin Watts, 1973.

Cerami, Charles A. *Jefferson's Great Gamble.*
Naperville, IL: Sourcebooks, 2003.

Colbert, David, editor. *Eyewitness to America.*
New York: Vintage, 1998.

Fleming, Thomas. *The Louisiana Purchase.*
New York: Alfred A. Knopf, 2003.

Kukla, Jon. *A Wilderness So Immense.*
New York: John Wiley and Sons, 2003.

New Orleans Museum of Art. *Jefferson's America and Napoléon's France.*
Seattle, Washington: University of Washington Press, 2003.

New Orleans Museum of Art. *Jefferson, Napoléon, and the Letter that Bought a Continent.*

New Orleans: New Orleans Museum of Art, 2003.

Relive other Milestones in history.

A Three-Minute Speech:

Lincoln's Remarks at Gettysburg

By Jennifer Armstrong

Illustrated by Albert Lorenz

Nellie Bly:

A Name to Be Reckoned With

By Stephen Krensky

Illustrated by Rebecca Guay

Cesar Chavez:

A Hero for Everyone

By Gary Soto

Illustrated by Lori Lohstoeter

Hard Labor:

The First African-Americans, 1619

By Patricia C. McKissack and

Frederick L. McKissack Jr.

Illustrated by Joseph Daniel

Fiedler

The Alamo

By Shirley Raye Redmond

Illustrated by Dominick Saponaro

Are You
Ready-for-Chapters 🫖

Page-turning step-up books for kids ready to tackle
something more challenging than beginning readers

The Cobble Street Cousins
by Cynthia Rylant
illustrated by
Wendy Anderson Halperin
#1 In Aunt Lucy's Kitchen
0-689-81708-8

#2 A Little Shopping
0-689-81709-6

#3 Special Gifts
0-689-81715-0

The Werewolf Club
by Daniel Pinkwater
illustrated by Jill Pinkwater
#1 The Magic Pretzel
0-689-83790-9

#2 The Lunchroom of Doom
0-689-83845-X

Third-Grade Detectives
by George Edward Stanley
illustrated by
Salvatore Murdocca
#1 The Clue of the Left-Handed Envelope
0-689-82194-8

#2 The Puzzle of the Pretty Pink Handkerchief
0-689-82232-4

Annabel the Actress:
Starring in Gorilla My Dreams
by Ellen Conford
illustrated by
Renee W. Andriani
0-689-83883-2

The Courage of Sarah Noble
by Alice Dalgliesh
0-689-71540-4

The Bears on Hemlock Mountain
by Alice Dalgliesh
0-689-71604-4

Ready-for-Chapters

ALADDIN PAPERBACKS
Simon & Schuster Children's Publishing • www.SimonSaysKids.com